HARRISON IN THE
ABBEY

Editor	**Arnold Wolfendale, Physics Department, Durham University, UK.**
Graphic Design	**Pauline Russell, Physics Department, Durham University, UK.**
Printed by	**Prontaprint, Durham.**
Sponsored by	**Smith of Derby Group Ltd.**

Arnold Wolfendale asserts the moral right
to be identified as the author of this book.

ISBN 1-904499-06-6

Further copies of this book may be obtained from:
The Clerk
The Worshipful Company of Clockmakers
Salters' Hall
Fore Street
London EC2Y 5DE

Tel : (020-7638-5500)
e-mail : clockmakersco@aol.com

 First published in United Kingdom of Great Britain in 2006 by Roundtuit
Publishing, 32 Cookes Wood, Broompark, Durham DH7 7RL

Printed in the United Kingdom of Great Britain by Prontaprint Durham.

Contents

Every seaman knows the vital necessity to determine a ship's position accurately when it is out of sight of land. The problem of finding a ship's latitude – north or south of the equator – was solved hundreds of years ago. Establishing a ship's longitude – that is its position east or west of a given position on land – defied solution until John Harrison designed and made a timekeeper that was sufficiently accurate and reliable. It took him most of his life to get his solution officially adopted, but every seaman – and airman – since that time has had cause to be grateful to Harrison. This memorial, here in Westminster Abbey, is a long overdue national tribute to the brilliant achievement of this remarkable man.

Philip

His Royal Highness, Prince Philip
Duke of Edinburgh.

Introduction

Arnold Wolfendale

Westminster Abbey, a magnificent building over one thousand years old, is Britain's premier 'church' and the shrine to many of the good and the great of the past. Here one will find memorials to priests, military men, statesmen, artists, musicians, poets, engineers, scientists and others. The horologist will beat a path to the grave of the 'Father of English clock and watch making', Thomas Tompion (1639-1713), whose grave also includes that of his colleague and successor, George Graham FRS (1674-1751). Not far away is a simple tablet in the floor of the nave commemorating Robert Hooke FRS (1635-1703) the brilliant scientist-cum-inventor who also contributed greatly to horology. Interestingly, Hooke was Surveyor to the Abbey and to the City, amongst many other appointments.

There is now added (24 March 2006) a simple memorial to John Harrison (1693-1776) honouring the man who overcame unbelievable difficulties to produce a sea-going clock with which longitude could be determined at sea to much greater accuracy than hitherto. The accuracy was such as to enable Harrison to effectively win the Longitude Prize of 1714. This Prize, of the phenomenal sum, for those days, of £20,000, was eagerly sought by many, using a variety of techniques, but it was Harrison who overcame the odds, and triumphed.

This commemorative book is published to mark the occasion of the unveiling of the memorial in the Abbey, and to act as a tribute to this *remarkable man. It is also a vehicle to encourage further donations to 'the Harrison Memorial Fund'. The brochure contains significant articles about John Harrison and his work and its significance by John Taylor, Dava Sobel, Will Andrewes and Andrew King. It also includes notes about the Abbey, the memorial itself, the Clockmakers' Museum and, importantly, the Worshipful Company of Clockmakers (by the Master, for 2005, Diana Uff). It was the Company which mounted the Appeal for funds to cover the cost of the memorial.*

Before embarking on these topics it is relevant briefly to trace the history of the project. The author, as the 14th Astronomer Royal and also an Honorary Liveryman of the Clockmakers' Company and President of the Antiquarian Horological Society, is obviously interested in 'time', its measurement and its significance, and had long been aware of the importance of Harrison's work, but it was Dava Sobel's now famous book, 'Longitude', published in 1995, that focused attention on the activities of the 5th Astronomer Royal, Nevil Maskelyne in the saga. Whilst certainly not going so far as Ms Sobel in her castigation of Maskelyne, who was also after the Longitude Prize himself, it seems clear that his support of Harrison (of the sort that a predecessor, Edmond Halley, had given) was, to say the least, inadequate. On enquiring as to how Harrison was formally commemorated in the nation, it appeared that he was not. Remedial action was clearly indicated.

The Worshipful Company of Clockmakers graciously initiated a 'Harrison Medal' in perpetuity, 'to commemorate outstanding achievements in propagating knowledge of the history of clockmaking and its appreciation'. The first winner was Jonathan Betts (2002) and the second Dava Sobel (2004); both have contributed to this book.

The next idea was to investigate the possibility of a commemorative memorial in the Abbey. There are many precedents for long delays in honouring long-dead luminaries: Robert Hooke had to wait 302 years after his death (the memorial was unveiled by the then President of The Royal Society, Lord May of Oxford, in 2005); even Shakespeare had to wait 124 years. The delay for Harrison was to be 230 years – almost the average of the two!

The Dean of the Abbey at the time, the Very Reverend Dr. Wesley Carr, proved very receptive to the idea, and most cooperative, and plans were laid. The Receiver-General, Major-General David Burden and the Surveyor to the Abbey, Mr. John Burton (a worthy successor to Robert Hooke) also played important parts.

The details of the memorial and its inscription are outlined later in the article by Jonathan Betts and notes on the Appeal and a list of the major donors are

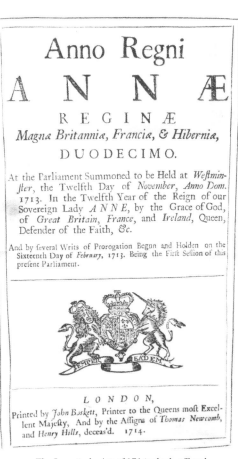

The Longitude Act of 1714 which offered the Longitude Prize of £20,000.

given by the Clerk to the Clockmakers, Joe Buxton.

The article on the Clockmakers' Museum, by Sir George White, also describes the role of the Clockmakers' Company in the Harrison saga and various items held in the Collection.

The income from the sale of this book will be passed to the Fund.

The Editor apologies for the inevitable repetitions from time to time in the articles; hopefully they do not detract from the story.

The Editor thanks the contributors for their ready cooperation and erudition.

We are grateful to Mr. J N W Smith whose clockmaking Company (Smith of Derby Group Ltd.) funded production of the book as part of their 150th anniversary celebrations. Fascinatingly, the Company formerly occupied the early home of the First Astronomer Royal, John Flamsteed (AR:1675-1719) in Derby. Equally interesting is the responsibility of the Company for the clock in the great North West tower of the Abbey shown on the cover of this book.

Finally, in this introduction, it is a pleasure and an honour to recognize the kindness shown by Prince Philip, Duke of Edinburgh, in agreeing to unveil the Harrison Memorial. The Prince, a naval man, knows better than most the contribution of John Harrison to ensuring that the British Navy 'ruled the waves'.

Jet Lag

"Time is to clock as mind is to brain."
Dava Sobel in Longitude (1996)

Most of the time my age fits me exactly.
The clock on my wrist keeps time
*   with the clock inside me;*
The seconds pile up minutely into days,
Thickening into wrinkles of sundays and mondays,
*   sunny days, moony days.*
So Time passes within me and through me,
Conveying me on its slow-moving walkway
Out of the duty-free clap trap of the airport
Into the desert of a new dimension
*   where it ionizes and splits up.*

If, from my choice meridian, I decide to fly
Westward through the lines of longitude,
I'll spring into New York or Boston
*   five hours younger;*
If eastward to Islamabad or Almaty, I'll arrive
Sleepless, in a grouchy mood, five hours older.
Meantime, my ticking pulse will punish me
*   for being alive,*
For keeping my home time going like Harrison's clock,
Mechanical, reliable, but in life's time, unpredictable,
*   like sailor's luck.*

Anne Stevenson

Westminster Abbey and its Memorials

Arnold Wolfendale

*A*s is often the case with abbeys and cathedrals, and indeed with most religious foundations, there were religious buildings present before the existing one. Westminster Abbey is no exception and it seems that there have been Christian communities on the site for twelve hundred years, and perhaps longer.

Westminster Abbey was a Benedictine monastery from the tenth century to the sixteenth, when it was surrendered to the crown. Records go back to the tenth century, and are extensive from the thirteenth. An Act of Parliament named the building as a cathedral church in the diocese of London and the first Dean was William Benson (Dean from 1540-49), the man who had been Abbot of the monastery from 1533-40.

The present Collegiate Church has a foundation charter which dates from 21 May 1560; remarkably it is exempt from the Archbishop of Canterbury and the Bishop of London.

An example of the significance of the Abbey is the fact that it has been the site of the coronation of all the crowned sovereigns of England since William I, William being crowned on Christmas Day, 1066. Another is its role as a final resting place for royalty.

Turning to its memorials, and graves, for which it is truly noted, the Reformation marked a turning point when emphasis moved to include commemorating the famous, in many walks of life, as well as those who had served the Abbey. The Abbey is now regarded as a national shrine and it has a special place in the hearts of the British. Pride of place must go to the Grave of the Unknown Warrior, a soldier whose body was brought back from France just two years after the end of the First

Newton's tomb and Memorial.

World War (on 11 November 1920). Nearby is the memorial to Winston Churchill, the statesman, author and wartime leader.

Moving East towards the altar, the grave of the 'horological giants' Thomas Tompion (1639-1713) and George Graham (1674-1751) is quickly reached and it is adjacent to this grave that John Harrison's memorial is situated – a clearly appropriate place.

Sir Isaac Newton PRS.

It is fascinating to look at other memorials in the Abbey, some of them nearby, which have relevance to the Harrison story. Pride of place is given to the great monument to Isaac Newton (1642-1727). Newton was 'implicated' in the story because of his strongly held view that an astronomical method was the only way forward for determining longitude at sea – to achieve sufficient accuracy using a sea-borne clock was to him clearly too difficult. It was Newton's advice to the then newly formed Board of Longitude, favouring an astronomical method, that made Harrison's task harder and his eventual success so much more remarkable. Newton was a friend and associate of Edmond Halley (1656-1742); indeed, Halley, who became the second Astronomer Royal (1720-42), not only primed

Edmond Halley FRS, 2nd Astronomer Royal.

Newton with astronomical problems to solve, but also paid for the publication of Newton's epic 'Principia'. Halley's impressive memorial is in the Cloisters. It was Halley, however, who introduced the 37-year old Harrison, who had such original horological ideas, to the brilliant scientist and instrument maker, George Graham, now, in the Abbey, a 'near-neighbour'. George Graham was a 'power in the land' and his help — including a loan — was invaluable.

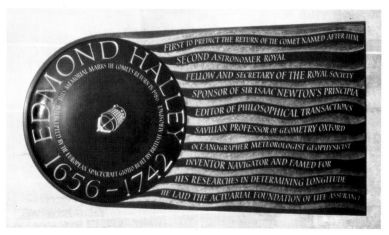

The Halley memorial in the Cloisters.

At first sight, a large monument by Grinling Gibbons in the South Choir Aisle might be thought of as irrelevant. In fact, it is very relevant. The edifice is over the tomb of Admiral Sir Clowdisley Shovell (1650-1707) and it was he who, after a distinguished career, through inaccurate navigation ran his flagship and three others on to the rocks of the Scilly Isles in 1707. Approaching two thousand died, including the Admiral, although he reputedly survived the shipwreck but was murdered on the beach at Porthellick Cove for his emerald ring.

This event and many other nautical disasters led to the famous 1714 Longitude Act in the reign of Queen Anne, offering the huge prize of £20,000 for a method to determine longitude at sea to a prescribed accuracy. This, then, was the Prize that John Harrison sought and effectively won.

To end on a royal note, Queen Anne died in the year of the Act and is herself buried in the Abbey in the magnificent Chapel of King Henry VII.

John Harrison's Early Wooden Clocks

John C. Taylor

arton upon Humber is a rural area today even with the Humber Bridge a couple of miles to the West of the town. At the beginning of the Eighteenth Century, as John Harrison was growing up, it was one of the most remote regions of England. No clocks are described as being by a local clockmaker and it appears unlikely that there was a skilled craftsman locally to advise Harrison. As only 50 years had passed since the invention of the pendulum clock in Holland by Huygens, and its introduction into London by Fromanteel, it is likely that few of these expensive luxuries were owned locally.

However, if any local clock owner had a problem, it is the very remoteness of the area that would have mitigated against sending the clock away for service thereby providing a need for someone locally with a little knowledge or the bravado to undertake the job of getting the mechanism going again. Perhaps Harrison was the man to raise his head above the parapet to have a go? This may be how Harrison gained an insight into the workings of clocks and set out to make his own.

John Harrison's early wooden clocks fall into three groups with progression of innovation continuing throughout their production.

$\mathcal{T}$he recoil anchor clocks from c1713

From Harrison's later work one would expect that these early examples too would be brim full of inventions: here innovation is in the detail. From a twenty-first century perspective, they do indeed appear remarkable and innovative: they are constructed almost entirely of oak — the material of his craftsmanship as a carpenter.

Harrison's first wooden clock.

Many of the early clocks made by the Fromanteels had the brass front plate divided in two parts so that each train could be worked on independently. In his first wooden clock Harrison followed exactly in the traditions of the finest London clockmakers; he formed the wooden backplate in two sections to enable the striking and going trains to be inserted and worked on separately.

Harrison assembled the wheels from oak sections cut along the grain and nested together like pieces of pie, ensuring each tooth was strong

The reverse of the first wooden clock, showing the separate striking and going trains.

and not across the grain. He cut his gear teeth in a conventional tooth form, aiming to give rolling friction. The wheels were glued onto boxwood arbors with integral cut pinions and inserted steel ends. Brass bearings were inserted in the wooden plates so the construction reflected a metal clock made mostly in wood. The sole metal wheel is the brass escapewheel engaged by the pair of pallets from a curved forged iron anchor escapement of conventional form. Nearly 300 years later there

Harrison's forged iron anchor escapement.

is virtually no wear in the bearings and remarkably little on the oak wheels or on the wood pinions.

'Little wear after nearly 300 years'!

Unfortunately, all the cases of the three extant clocks have been lost and we have no idea how Harrison housed and displayed the results of his first foray into clockmaking.

$\mathcal{T}$he Brocklesby Park Tower Clock c1722.

By 1720 Harrison had established a sufficient reputation as a clockmaker to be commissioned by Sir Charles Pelham to build a tower clock for his newly constructed Stable Block at his country seat of Brocklesby Park. The general concept of this tower clock was similar to his earlier domestic clocks: an enlarged cross-tenonned oak frame with inserted wooden plates for the mechanism. Harrison appreciated that his wooden gears could shrink as the wood dried out, thereby destroying the pitch circle diameter and tooth engagement with increasing friction. He used beautifully cut brass pinions throughout, except for the escapewheel pinion, made with a ring of little rollers to reduce friction. The rollers rotated on thin brass bearings running in brass rings reminiscent of a lantern. He redesigned the main bearings with self lubricating *lignum vitae* bushes in which ran the brass pivots without the need for additional oil.

The fundamental difference between a tower clock and a domestic clock is the requirement to turn the large minute and hour hands on the tower from the clock in the loft below. This requires the output shaft to be turned through a right angle and taken up to the upper level of the clock face, turned back horizontally and then also geared down from the minute shaft

The 'lantern' roller pinion.

12:1 for the hour hand. Thus, considerable driving force is needed because of all the friction in the many extra gears and bearings. The excess drive must be absorbed in the friction of the anchor escapement and a larger swing. The original escapement installed was an enlarged version of his anchor escapement design with the innovative improvement of inserted pallets.

Harrison may have underestimated the additional problems of the wind either helping the exposed hands round the dial or trying to stop the clock, or even a pair of pigeons alighting on the minute hand when horizontal! Also, the temperature variations in the unheated draughty clock loft made the oil or goose grease go thick instead of lubricating the sliding friction between the pallets and the escapewheel through the change in its viscosity. After installation, the clock proved unreliable and Harrison had to make many unpaid visits to try to make the clock keep running as designed and keep time.

With true innovative genius Harrison devised a new type of escapement that had pivoted pallets and no sliding friction to the escapewheel. Thus, no lubrication of any sort was required. This new mechanism, nicknamed a "*grasshopper*" as it appeared to hop round the escapewheel, gave more impulse to the swing of the pendulum and increased its arc.

Clockmakers had spent many years trying to reduce this amplitude to improve accuracy and timekeeping and Harrison was now faced with a large increase and a variation in amplitude. Surprisingly, a pendulum swinging with a large arc appears to go faster than one with a small arc but actually goes slower; the laws of physics dictate poor timekeeping with variable amplitude.

Unknown to Harrison, the requirement for a constant time of swing had been solved by the designer of the first pendulum clock: Christiaan Huygens. Both men independently came up with the same empirical solution: as the pendulum amplitude increases, reduce the length of the pendulum so that the time of the swing remains constant. This was done with curved cheeks touching the pendulum spring suspension so that the

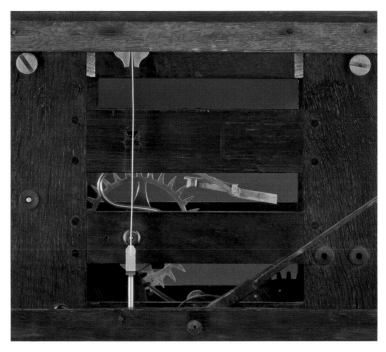

*At the top of the pendulum suspension spring the (slightly) curved cheeks can
be seen, with half the grasshopper escapement visible mid way down.*

apparent length of the pendulum decreased as the swing increased and
thereby achieved an isochronous result regardless of amplitude.

Instead of using a traditional streamlined bob, Harrison fitted a vane
behind his heavy bob to dissipate some of the excess energy required to
drive the motion work.   The bigger arc of swing created by the
grasshopper escapement, extra driving weights and the variations caused
by the wind (and pigeons!), were cancelled out by the constant time
properties of the pendulum with the isochronous cheeks.

Domestic Regulators from c1725

It is a subject of conjecture as to how John Harrison first heard of the Longitude Prize, but in any event before attempting to make a sea clock he needed an accurate land clock against which to judge the performance of any new concept, such as one without a pendulum which would be of little use on a rolling ship. With the tribulations of Brocklesby behind him, he was able to design a series of accurate clocks incorporating all the improvements he had made and create further innovations. His younger brother, James, joined him in the construction of the clocks and it is James' name that appears on the dials. To defray the development costs, it appears that he planned to make a series of about half a dozen domestic regulators. He kept two for himself to compare the results as he tried further innovations and he sold on the others.

The basic construction details were retained in the oak frame with inserted front and back plates but no ferrous material was used in the mechanism, brass was chosen for all the shafts and the bearings were of self lubricating *lignum vitae*. For the important bearings of the escapewheel a pair of rollers was used to further reduce friction. The brass escapewheel was retained but the grasshopper escapement redesigned with the two pallets pivoting on a single gold wire shaft. Most important of all: the pendulum was temperature compensated.

At this time the expansion of metals was known but nothing had been measured absolutely. Harrison discovered that the expansion of brass was more then that of steel and that the hardness and type of brass affected the expansion. By using a central steel rod, and then on each side alternate steel and brass rods folded back on themselves, the expansion of the steel rods was nullified by the expansion of the brass rods so that the overall length of the composite pendulum rod remained

Looking down on the escapewheel and its two supporting rollers.

constant with change of temperature.   The parallel rods looked like a gridiron.

To confirm the long term accuracy and stability in his clocks, Harrison needed an accurate time base far better than given by a sundial. A good sundial can be carefully read to the nearest minute but must be corrected by the *'equation of time'*. Harrison needed to check to better than a second and claimed to be able to read his clock to a twentieth part of a second by watching the pendulum. For his time base he used a star transit: watching for a star to be occulted by his neighbour's chimney against

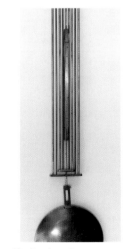

The 'gridiron' temperature compensated pendulum.

his own cottage window. He then waited until the next evening when that star came by and was again occulted with an exact time interval of 23 hours 56 minutes and 4.09 seconds. This simple practical method showed Harrison at his most innovative.

The final results were the most accurate clocks ever made anywhere in the World to that date and remained so for 100 years.

With such a good result, Harrison was emboldened to travel to London to explain his ideas and seek financial help to make a prototype sea clock. Of the many elite he met, none was more important to his cause than George Graham who was at the height of his fame as a Fellow of The Royal Society, a horologist and instrument maker. Harrison must have sounded crazy when he talked to Graham about his accuracy of a second a month but was reluctant to explain how this was achieved. A good Graham clock kept to a second a day!

Happily, Graham was true to precepts and he persisted, trying to understand and create a meeting of minds. He immediately recognised the elegant solution of Harrison in his Grid Iron as Graham too had tried to make a temperature compensated pendulum: so far he had failed. Graham was so impressed with the results that Harrison obtained from his early wooden clocks that he became one of Harrison's most loyal and generous supporters.

Harrison's wooden clocks were accurate to better than 1 second per month and would run for 40 to 50 years without maintenance. They established many of the principles that ended with H4 showing the World that a clock solution of the Longitude Problem was feasible.

Harrison the Man

Dava Sobel

The man honoured in the Abbey, on 24 March 2006 — 313 years to the day after his birth in Foulby, Yorkshire, and 230 years (also to the day) after his death in London — would no doubt be pleased to find his memorial so close to two men he sincerely admired in his lifetime: George Graham and Thomas Tompion. John "Longitude" Harrison, clockmaker of Barrow, first met George Graham in 1730, when he showed him the plans for the first of his sea clocks designed to solve the problem of the longitude. As Harrison described their encounter,

> *"Mr. Graham began as I thought very roughly with me, and the which had like to have occasioned me to become rough too; but however we got the ice broke . . . and indeed he became as at last vastly surprised at the thoughts or methods I had taken."*

At the time of that historic meeting, Graham was London's premier instrument maker and a Fellow of The Royal Society. Harrison was the village carpenter in Barrow-on-Humber, in Lincolnshire, an auto-didact who had schooled himself by reading and copying a manuscript of lectures Nicholas Saunderson delivered at Cambridge. A sometimes viol player who rang and tuned the church bells and led the parish choir, Harrison had completed his first pendulum clock before he reached twenty years of age. Why he chose to take on that project, and how he excelled at it with no experience as a watchmaker's apprentice, remain mysteries.

The movement and dial of Harrison's first clock — signed, dated fossils from his formative period — can still be seen at The Worshipful Company of Clockmakers' Museum in Guildhall. Aside from the fact that the great John Harrison built it, that first clock claims uniqueness for another singular feature: it is constructed almost entirely of wood — truly a carpenter's clock, with oak wheels and boxwood axles connected and impelled by small amounts of brass and steel.

George Graham FRS, the noted instrument maker, who befriended Harrison.

A tale, probably apocryphal, holds that Harrison once sustained himself through a childhood illness by listening to the ticking of a pocket watch laid upon his pillow. Even if his family could have afforded such a luxury, which is doubtful, they could not have found a ready source. No known clockmaker, other than self-taught Harrison himself, lived or worked anywhere around north Lincolnshire in the early eighteenth century.

On August 30, 1718, Harrison married Elizabeth Barrel. Their son, John, was born the following summer. Later, Elizabeth fell ill and died in the spring before the boy turned seven. The parish records show that Harrison found a new bride, ten years younger, within six months of Elizabeth's death. Harrison wed his second wife, Elizabeth Scott, on

November 23, 1726. At the start of their fifty years together they had two children: William, born in 1728, who was to become his father's right-hand man and champion, and Elizabeth, born in 1732, about whom nothing is known save for the date of her baptism, December 21. John, the child of Harrison's first marriage, died when he was only eighteen.

Sometime around 1720, after Harrison had built another two long case clocks and gained something of a reputation as a maker, Sir Charles Pelham hired him to build a tower clock above the stable at his manor house in Brocklesby Park. Harrison completed that commission about 1722, and the clock still tells time today. It has been running continuously for more than 280 years, except for a brief period in 1884 when workers stopped it for refurbishing. The clock never needs lubrication because the parts that would

Brocklesby Park - Harrison's 1722 clock.
above the stables.

normally call for it were carved out of *lignum vitae*, a tropical hardwood that exudes its own grease. Aside from avoiding the need for oil, Harrison also avoided the use of iron or steel anywhere in the clockwork, for fear it would rust in the damp conditions. Wherever he needed metal, he installed parts made of brass.

As he built additional clocks, Harrison teamed up with his brother James, eleven years his junior but, like him, a superb craftsman. From 1725 to 1727 the brothers built two long-case clocks. James Harrison signed them both in bold script right on their painted wood faces. The name John Harrison does not appear anywhere, outside or inside, though there is not a horologist in the world who doubts that John was the designer and driving force in the construction of these clocks, which include two of his precision inventions, the "gridiron" pendulum and the "grasshopper" escapement.

The Harrison brothers tested the accuracy of their gridiron-grasshopper clocks against the regular motions of the stars, using the homemade astronomical transit instrument described previously by John Taylor. In their late-night tests, their clocks never erred more than a single *second* in a whole *month*, while the very finest quality watches being produced anywhere in the world at that time drifted off by about one *minute* every *day*.

By the year 1727, Harrison recalled late in life, visions of the £20,000 Longitude Prize had turned his mind to the special challenge of marine timekeeping. After nearly four years spent devising the innovations that would make his fine clocks seaworthy, he traveled the two hundred miles from Barrow to London and laid his plan before the Board of Longitude. This blue-ribbon panel, created by the Longitude Act of 1714, consisted of admirals, scientists, and members of Parliament. Edmond Halley, the second Astronomer Royal at Greenwich, served as an ex officio member, and it was he who first entertained Harrison's idea.

Impressed with the design for the first sea clock, Halley referred Harrison to Graham, who received his ideas enthusiastically and also advanced him a generous loan to help get the project under way. Harrison then spent the next five years piecing together what has since come to be known as "H-1," and testing it on a barge on the River Humber. In 1735 he carried it to London, and made good on his promise to Graham.

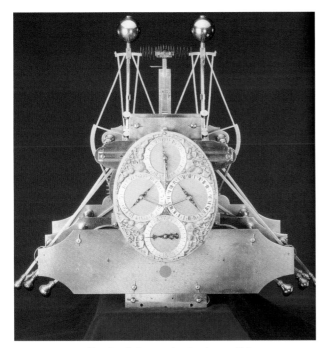

Harrison's first marine timekeeper H-1.

In 1736, H-1 was sent on a sea trial that carried it and its maker on a one-week voyage to Lisbon, Portugal. Harrison, plagued with seasickness, suffered all the way there and no doubt more so on the month-long journey back. But when land was sighted at last, Harrison was able to correct the ship's position by the time shown on his clock. Although the navigator had taken their position to be the Start, near Dartmouth, Harrison argued it was the Lizard on the Penzance peninsula, and he was right. This triumph led, one year later, to the first-ever meeting of the Board of Longitude. Twenty-three years after its creation by the Longitude Act of 1714, the Board finally had something worthy of the consideration of its commissioners.

Harrison himself, however, did not think H-1 deserved the Prize. He asked the Board, which functioned as the world's first research-and-development agency, to advance him £500 toward the construction of a second, improved timekeeper. The commissioners agreed to do this, with a promise of another £500 upon completion of the instrument. However, when Harrison appeared before them in 1741 with the finished H-2, which had already been warmly endorsed by The Royal Society, he himself rejected it. The same viselike conviction that led him to his finest mechanisms — along his own lines of thinking, without regard for the opinions of others — rendered him deaf to praise. All he wanted was to go home and try again.

Harrison, now a London resident, forty-eight years of age, faded into his workshop in Red Lion Square and was hardly heard from during the nearly two decades he devoted to the completion of his "curious third machine." He emerged periodically to request and collect from the Board of Longitude occasional stipends of £500, as he slogged through the difficulties of transforming the bar-shaped balances of the first two timekeepers into the circular balance wheels that graced the third.

Lieutenant Commander Rupert T. Gould of the Royal Navy, who undertook the repair and restoration of Harrison's sea clocks in 1920, said of the third timekeeper, "No. 3 is not merely complicated, like No. 2, it is abstruse. It embodies several devices which are entirely unique — devices which no clockmaker has ever thought of using, and which Harrison invented as the result of tackling his mechanical problems as an engineer might, and not as a clockmaker would."

Harrison left his workbench long enough to accept the Copley Gold Medal from The Royal Society — the highest tribute its members could confer. The members also offered him Fellowship in the Society, but he declined to join.

In a retrospective review of his career milestones, Harrison wrote of the hard lessons he had learned from H-3. Among its 753 parts lie innovations that can still be found today in worldwide industrial use. However H-3, like H-2 before it, never underwent a trial at sea.

While Harrison worked, astronomers perfected their own technique for finding the longitude,

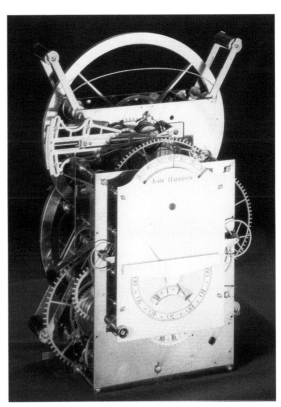

Harrison's H-3.

which they called "taking lunars" or the lunar-distance method. It made use of the Moon's motion against the background stars as a celestial indicator of time. Contributions by several individuals over many years produced the theories, instruments, and predictions that made lunars practicable by the late 1750s. And it was in the year 1759 that Harrison completed his masterpiece, the fourth timekeeper, H-4.

Harrison, who had always been his own worst critic, truly loved H-4.

"I think I may make bold to say," he wrote, "that there is neither any other Mechanical or Mathematical thing in the World that is more beautiful or curious in texture than this my watch or Timekeeper for the Longitude . . . and I heartily thank Almighty God that I have lived so long, as in some measure to complete it."

William Harrison, though a child when the work on the sea clocks began, had passed through his teens and twenties in the company of H-3, and it was he who carried H-4, his father's Watch, on its official trial to Jamaica in October of 1761. When the ship made landfall at Port Royal, H-4 had lost only five seconds in eighty-one days at sea. Its performance on the journey home through rough waters was equally impressive, but the Board of Longitude took a hard line on these results. In fact, in August 1762, the Board insisted on a second trial. Though the Harrisons angrily objected to this request, William set out again in March of 1764, bound for Barbados with H-4. The Watch's second trial proved just as successful as the first; nevertheless the results failed to convince the Board of Longitude that Harrison deserved the Prize.

The spring of 1765 brought a new Longitude Act from Parliament, which named Harrison in its opening language and described the current status of his contrariety with the Board. It stipulated that Harrison must build two additional timekeepers identical to H-4, as proof that his invention was truly "practicable and useful." Harrison, meanwhile, stormed out of more than one Board meeting, and was heard swearing that he would not comply with the outrageous demands foisted on him *"so long as he had a drop of English blood in his body."*

Later that summer, beginning on August 14, 1765, Harrison submitted to a *'disclosure proceeding,'* in which he took apart H-4 and fully explained its complexities to a committee of expert mathematicians and watchmakers. This ordeal lasted six days. When it was over, the Board of Longitude insisted that Harrison reassemble the Watch and surrender it to the Admiralty, where it awaited. In exchange for his cooperation, Harrison received £10,000.

Sometime between October 1765 and March 1766, Harrison sat for the formal portrait in oils by Thomas King that now hangs in the Royal Observatory at Greenwich (and is shown on the cover of this book). Dressed in chocolate brown frock coat and breeches, he is surrounded by his inventions. Behind him are H-3 and the precision gridiron-pendulum regulator, which he built to rate his other timepieces. Though seated, he assumes an erect bearing and a look of self-satisfied, but not smug, accomplishment. He wears a gentleman's white wig and has the clearest, smoothest skin imaginable. His blue eyes, though a bit rheumy at seventy-plus years of age, direct a level gaze. Only the eyebrows, raised at the center, and the lines between them, betray the

Harrison's prize-winning watch H-4.

man's cautious craftsmanship, his nagging concerns. He holds his left arm akimbo, hand on hip. His right forearm rests on a table, and in his right hand is the small pocket watch that he had asked John Jefferys to make for him, incorporating Harrison's own temperature-compensation device. The accuracy of this watch had inspired Harrison to jump from his three large sea clocks, which all stood at least two feet tall and weighed in the neighborhood of eighty pounds, to the petite H-4, only five inches in diameter and three pounds in weight. H-4 itself does not appear in the portrait, because Harrison no longer had it in his possession.

In April of 1766, in order to put to rest all lingering doubts that H-4's accuracy might be chalked up to chance or luck, the Board decided to subject the timekeeper to a new sort of trial at the Royal Observatory, where it went through daily tests over a period of ten months. At the same time, Harrison was made to turn in the three large sea clocks as well, for they had become *"the property of the public."* Porters removing the clocks from Harrison's house, accidentally dropped H-1 as they carried it down the steps. Adding to this ignominy, the clocks were wheeled all the way to Greenwich in an unsprung cart.

Harrison soon got to work on the reproductions of H-4 that the new Longitude Act required of him. By 1770 — despite his ill treatment, advanced age, failing eyesight, and periodic bouts of gout — he finished the first of the pair. This timekeeper, now known as H-5, has all the internal complexity of H-4, but assumes a more austere outward appearance, with no frills on its dial or fancy engraving on its backplate. Having built this watch in three years, Harrison tested and adjusted it for another two. By the time it pleased him, he was seventy-nine. He did not see how he could now start another project of equal proportions. Even if he completed the work, the official trials might extend into the next decade, though his life surely could not. This sense of being backed against the wall, without hope of justice, emboldened him to tell his troubles to the King.

His Majesty King George III took an active interest in science, and had followed the trials of H-4. He had even granted John and William Harrison an audience when H-4 returned from its first voyage to Jamaica. In January 1772 William wrote to the King to request that H-5 **"be lodged for a certain time in the Observatory at Richmond in order to ascertain and manifest its degree of excellence."**

King George III (1738-1820).

According to an account written in 1835 by William's son, John, the King interviewed William at length at Windsor Castle, and muttered under his breath, **"These people have been cruelly treated."** *Aloud he promised William,* **"By God, Harrison, I will see you righted!"**

True to his word, George III turned over H-5 to his private Observatory director for indoor trials that lasted ten weeks. The timekeeper proved accurate to within one-third of one second per day. The King then helped the Harrisons circumvent the obdurate Board by appealing directly to the Prime Minister, Lord North, and to Parliament. At the King's suggestion, Harrison dropped the legal blustering that had marked his recent negotiations, and simply appealed to the hearts of the ministers. He was an old man. He had devoted his life to these endeavors. And although he had succeeded, he was rewarded with only half a prize plus new — and impossible — demands.

This approach carried the day. The final resolution took a few more weeks to go through channels, but at last, at the end of June, 1773, Harrison received £8,750. This amount nearly totaled the remainder of the Longitude Prize due him, though it was not the coveted Prize itself. Rather, the sum was a bounty awarded by the benevolence of Parliament — in spite of the Board of Longitude, instead of from it.

Harrison received considerable validation, however, from Captain James Cook, who had taken an exact replica of H-4 on his second voyage to the Pacific, and praised its performance without reservation upon his return to England in July, 1775.

With his marine clocks, John Harrison tested the waters of space-time. He succeeded, against all odds, at wresting the world's whereabouts from the stars, and locking the secret in a pocket watch. When he died on March 24, 1776, exactly eighty-three years of age, he was buried in the cemetery of St. John's Church, Hampstead. His wife, the second Elizabeth, and his son, William, are buried with him. The tomb was completely restored by The Worshipful Company of Clockmakers in 1879, and its engraved message tells the story of Harrison's historic work on the longitude problem.

Harrison's Contributions in Perspective

William Andrewes

Progress has little regard for the past. When John Harrison passed away on 24th March 1776, his work nearly perished with him. His three large longitude timekeepers were buried in the damp cellars of the Royal Observatory, forgotten like their maker, victims of time — the very dimension they had so lovingly been made to measure. Had this neglect continued until World War II, such cumbersome and dilapidated old relics might well have been discarded in the Royal Observatory's rapid move to escape the London air raids. In times of war — or even peace — what use is the past to the present?

Without the three large marine timekeepers, our appreciation and knowledge of Harrison's work would have become a footnote in history. We would stand in blind awe of H4, the secrets of its success too small and concealed for most to comprehend, unaware of the long succession of ideas that took timekeeping on land to sea. Their fate, however, became tied to that of a 30-year-old naval commander, Rupert Gould. Having been forced into early retirement after the First World War, Gould decided to write a history of the marine chronometer. Inevitably, this took him to Greenwich, where, on 5th March 1920, he found the sea-clocks in an appalling state. By the time of his death 28 years later, his painstaking restoration and eloquent prose had assured that Harrison's marine timekeepers would never again be forgotten. Their mesmerizing appearance has made them one of England's greatest national treasures. That little was known about Harrison's early work encouraged Humphrey

Quill, soon after his retirement in 1950 from a distinguished career in the Royal Marines, to take up where Gould had left off. Quill devoted his last 37 years to researching Harrison's life and work, discovering along the way several of his early wooden regulators. Following the 1966 publication of his biography, interest in Harrison spread rapidly. Martin

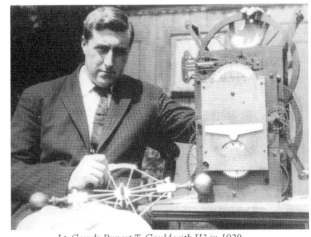

Lt. Comdr Rupert T. Gould with H3 in 1920.

Burgess, an artist-clockmaker, was inspired to use some of Harrison's ingenious ideas in his sculptural clocks and to establish a research group to advance our understanding of Harrison's technology. Bill Laycock, Andrew King, John Taylor, Jonathan Betts, and many others — including Dava Sobel, Arnold Wolfendale, and myself — have been captivated with this same consuming interest. Indeed, anyone who delves into Harrison's work cannot fail to be impressed.

Yet before the publicity and recognition of the last decade, many still regarded Harrison's work as an aberration. As significant as H4's performance was, what did the extraordinary mechanism he developed have to do with the advance of mainstream horology and technology? In his classic book on the history of the marine timekeeper, Gould had also praised the contributions of those following Harrison who, within 30 years, developed the modern marine chronometer. In a cursory observation, the only part of the chronometer that can be recognised as Harrison's invention is the maintaining power. Five vital elements, however, are easily overlooked. The first is its size. When Harrison embarked on his mission to solve the longitude problem with a timekeeper, no one had any idea how large such a mechanism should be. That it should be the size of a clock seemed too obvious to question, because clocks at that time were far more accurate and reliable than watches. The second is the speed of its controlling oscillator: the slow, seconds beat of a pendulum also seemed unquestionable, because pendulum clocks were the most precise timekeepers. Harrison himself pursued this path with his first three sea-clocks. However, during his nineteen-year struggle to perfect H3, his experiments with a watch with a small balance oscillating five times a second (its higher energy making it less affected by motion) led him to revolutionise his thinking and develop H4. The third element is Harrison's extensive use of pierced jewels for the pivot bearings. Jewelling was done at that time only in high quality English watches and its use was limited to only a few parts. After Harrison, the extensive use of pierced jewels became a standard feature in every high quality watch. The fourth relates to the advent of our reliance on technology: H4 was one of the first machines to which users entrusted their

Captain James Cook, FRS (1728-79)
Cook used a copy of H4 (called K1) as his primary
method of Navigation on his second voyage.

lives. Its exact copy, K1, went as a navigational aid on Captain Cook's second voyage. At the outset in 1772, Cook used it only as a back-up to his astronomical observations, but long before he returned to England in 1775, this small ticking machine had become his primary method of finding longitude at sea, charting his course as well as the coastlines of the islands he discovered. The fifth element in H4's contribution is the accomplishment itself. When Harrison began his quest, the very idea of making a clock to keep time at sea was considered impossible. No one had succeeded, not even the brilliant mathematician Christiaan Huygens, who had made the most significant advances in time measurement with his invention of the pendulum clock and the spiral balance spring for watches. Keeping time is one of the most demanding human endeavours. The seeming futility of even trying to solve the longitude problem with a timekeeper is revealed by the fact that, between 1730 and 1760, Harrison was alone in this endeavour. His success, however, immediately inspired several ingenious followers, who, by 1790, had developed the mechanical marine chronometer to such an advanced level that its basic design never changed. Harrison's complicated and sophisticated work was quickly outdated and considered to have no relevance to the future. One of the reasons we need history is to remind us of where we were, of our path to the present, and to give past concepts and ideas a new context for development.

Harrison's pursuit of precision timekeeping is characterised by a steady progression of ideas, one building on the other, and an uncompromising attitude toward anything that needed improvement. He knew that he had to perfect timekeeping on land before he could ever attempt it at sea. The accuracy he sought and achieved is impressive even today. In his era, it was beyond the limits of comprehension. He claimed in his 1730

Precision longcase clock, signed
'James Harrison 3rd 1728 Barrow'.
This clock was retained by John
Harrison throughout his life.

manuscript that by 1728 he had made two wooden clocks that kept time to a second a month. A second a day is one part in 86,400; in a month, this is one part in 2,600,000. Since such accuracy was not officially recorded until the 1890s, Harrison's claim sounds like a gross exaggeration, particularly for wooden clocks. Yet the ingenious scientific methods he describes have the ring of truth. As John Taylor has described, to time his clocks, he used his neighbour's chimney, which was some 75 feet away. By aligning its left side with the left side of the upright of his window frame, he could observe each night with considerable accuracy the moment that a particular star disappeared behind the chimney. Thus, without any special equipment, he regulated his clocks precisely by the daily rotation of the Earth relative to a fixed star, the same standard used by astronomers until the middle of the last century. About 1726, Harrison contrived a new type of pendulum with a gridiron of brass and steel rods, arranged in such a way that they compensated for the effects of temperature variation. Equally ingenious was his solution to combat changes in barometric pressure (which he called "weight of the air"), an effect on timekeeping that he could not have observed unless his clocks were extremely accurate. Harrison knew that, for a pendulum to swing in the same period of time regardless of the width of its arc, it has to travel in a cycloidal, not circular, path. By adjusting the suspension device that guided the pendulum in this motion and balancing this with careful alterations in the temperature compensation, he found that he could also negate the effects of barometric pressure. His attempts to eliminate friction by using a unique form of escapement (known by its action as the "Grasshopper"), by using the naturally oily wood called *lignum vitae* in every bearing and his use of specially designed roller pinions have already been described. The ensuing extraordinary advances in timekeeping on land, however, were highly unconventional and thus never met with the interest that might have led to their development as observatory timekeepers. As far as Harrison was concerned, their purpose was to solve the problem of keeping time on land and thereby establish the principles for designing a sea-clock.

To adapt his ideas for keeping time at sea, Harrison recognised that he would need to use metal rather than wood to achieve greater rigidity. However, as demonstrated by his invention of the gridiron pendulum, he selected metals as thoughtfully as wood. To minimise the use of ferrous metals, he developed alloys of tin and copper, adjusting the proportions to suit different purposes. His mechanisms were the result of thorough experimentation, the design of every part dictated by its function. The unusual appearance of his first three marine timekeepers, which may seem extraordinary at first sight, evolved from the function of their integral parts. Harrison took five years to develop and refine the concepts of his wooden regulators into his first marine timekeeper, H1. Although this timekeeper shines in appearance and innovation, its most influential invention was its automatic maintaining power (the device that keeps it running while being wound), which was widely adopted in precision timekeepers.

H1's trial voyage proved its worth, but did not satisfy its maker. To perform as it did, it needed constant supervision as well as a working knowledge of the mechanism. While everything looked so promising on the outside, Harrison knew that improvements had to be made. His move to London in 1737 gave him access to the finest craftsmen, many of whom he would have met through George Graham. That his second marine timekeeper (H2) — a more compact and complicated copy of H1 made almost entirely of brass — took him only two years to complete was due to the assistance he had with its construction. Advised by George Graham, Edmond Halley, and other eminent friends, Harrison knew that time was of the essence. The interest shown by The

Harrison's H-2.

Royal Society, many of whose Fellows supported Harrison in his endeavours, would not last forever. Indeed, one of the reasons he had such difficulty gaining the prize money is that his most influential supporters died during the 20 years that passed between the completion of H2 and H4.

To overcome problems observed in H1's performance, H2 incorporates several innovations. The design of its stopwork, the device that prevents the clock from being overwound, was so efficient, compact, and reliable that it was recently adopted to protect the optical components of an infrared spectrograph. Harrison's dedicated pursuit of scientific truth is demonstrated by the fact that, as soon as he realised the inherent fault of using balance arms instead of balance wheels as the timekeeping

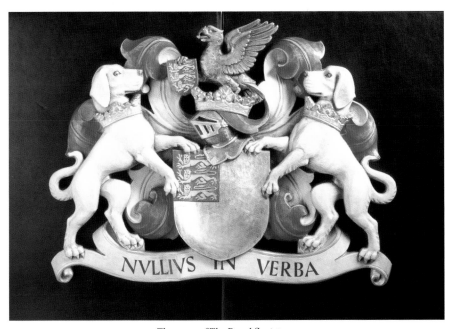

The arms of The Royal Society.

oscillators, he abandoned H2 and began construction of H3. During his nineteen-year struggle to perfect this machine he devised two components that would have an enduring impact on modern technology. The first was the bimetallic strip, which he invented to overcome the effects of temperature variation. This device, evolved from the principles of his gridiron pendulum, is widely used today in thermostat controls. The second was the caged roller bearing, which he developed from the antifriction rollers employed in his earlier timekeepers. This is the forerunner of the modern ball bearing used in a multitude of engineering applications. Harrison's work did not go unnoticed at the time: in 1749, he was granted the Copley Medal, the highest award of The Royal Society. H3 was never tested at sea, but it was a vital steppingstone to H4, the prize-winning watch.

The Copley Medal - The Royal Society's premier award - given to Harrison in 1749.

Although first and foremost scientific and technological, the longitude problem was also inextricably part of a larger nexus of law, politics, and empire building, of social and cultural history, and of commerce and economics. Improvements in navigation allowed not only safer but also more direct (and hence faster) passage across the oceans, resulting in greater intercontinental trade and the creation of new markets. The ability to chart geographic discoveries with ever-greater precision opened to European colonisation and development regions that hitherto had been

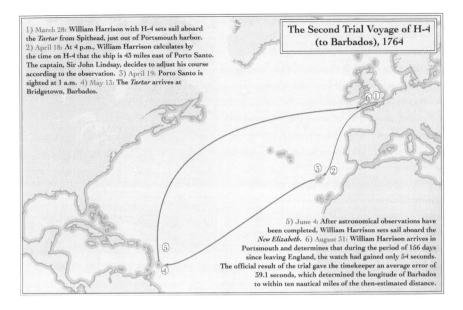

1) March 28: William Harrison with H-4 sets sail aboard the *Tartar* from Spithead, just out of Portsmouth harbor. 2) April 18: At 4 p.m., William Harrison calculates by the time on H-4 that the ship is 43 miles east of Porto Santo. The captain, Sir John Lindsay, decides to adjust his course according to the observation. 3) April 19: Porto Santo is sighted at 1 a.m. 4) May 13: The *Tartar* arrives at Bridgetown, Barbados.

The Second Trial Voyage of H-4 (to Barbados), 1764

5) June 4: After astronomical observations have been completed, William Harrison sets sail aboard the *New Elizabeth*. 6) August 31: William Harrison arrives in Portsmouth and determines that during the period of 156 days since leaving England, the watch had gained only 54 seconds. The official result of the trial gave the timekeeper an average error of 39.1 seconds, which determined the longitude of Barbados to within ten nautical miles of the then-estimated distance.

limited to explorers and pioneers. Subsequent discoveries of new plant and animal life greatly expanded the field of natural history, and the revelation of large deposits of gold and other natural resources led to commercial exploitation. These developments in turn caused massive shifts in population, significantly expanding the influence of some cultures while suppressing or even eradicating others. The enormous sums that had been invested in maritime enterprise began to pay off once the technique for determining longitude was available: for the next 150 years, Great Britain was the world's dominant naval power.

The story of how the longitude problem was solved — creating a massive financial incentive open to everyone — should not be overlooked. Perhaps one of the least obvious but most relevant of Harrison's contributions is that he proved the value of the individual: that someone with no university education or formal training in an associated field could solve one of the most daunting problems of his age.

The Worshipful Company of Clockmakers

Diana Uff

*J*ohn Harrison was not a member of the Worshipful Company of Clockmakers, but the Company has always recognised his remarkably important contribution to horology, and beyond. The Company introduced the 'Harrison Medal' which accelerated the drive to mark his work on the international stage. A further step has been the organisation of the present 'memorialisation' in Westminster Abbey. Harrison's contemporaries were members of the Clockmakers' Company and they both vied with and supported each other in the search for longitude and refined and developed his ideas after his final success.

The Editor of the book is pleased to include a description of the Worshipful Company in view of its importance in the development of horology over nearly four centuries, as well as its role in the present enterprise.

*T*he Worshipful Company of Clockmakers is one of the ancient Livery Companies of the City of London which, together with the more modern companies, presently number 107. The Clockmakers are 61 in the hierarchy of seniority, which depends on the date of the grant of the Charter. The Livery Companies grew out of the guilds or trade associations which were formed to protect craftsmen and their working practices. They were at the height of their power in the 15th and 16th centuries when crafts were very strictly controlled, but by the time the Clockmakers' received their Charter in 1631 the regime had started to become more liberal.

The oldest City Companies were concerned with the necessities of life, often associated with such staple trades as the Grocers, Bakers, Fishmongers, Weavers and Mercers, and at first often had religious links. As the wealth of the country increased, by the early 1600s, clocks and watches become every day items which could be afforded by ordinary people. At the same time, the business of the City of London began to require not only that time be measured, but measured with increasing accuracy. In England the earliest clocks were large turret clocks, found in churches or public buildings, made by clockmakers who were members of the Blacksmiths' Company because they were made for the most part of iron. Then, as there was more prosperity, increasing numbers of skilled craftsmen were drawn into the making of clocks, bringing with them new scientific and creative talents, such that clock and watch makers became a distinct group, anxious to assert their independence and to regulate their own activities.

The clockmakers then initiated the process which would lead them to obtain their own Charter. Pitfalls and discouragements lay ahead, not least from their former host company, the Blacksmiths. New applications for charters were viewed with jealousy and suspicion by the existing crafts and were frequently discouraged by the Court of Aldermen to which applications were referred by the King when he was petitioned to grant a charter. The Clockmakers' petition was finally granted by Charles I on 22 August 1631, admittedly at a time when the King was short of money as a result of the impending contest with Parliament. The Charter reads

> *'Know ye, that we (Charles, by the Grace of God, King of England...) at the humble petition of the Clockmakers, as well freemen of our city of London,....for the better order, rule and government of them...and others using the same*

Art or Mystery of Clockmaking...do will, ordain, constitute, declare and grant ...(the various freedoms contained in the Charter)'. It is signed *Wolseley.*

The word "Mystery" derives from the Latin 'ministerium' meaning occupation or craft, but also conveys a powerful image of the skills associated with the craft.

The Charter itself is engrossed on three large parchment skins, richly emblazoned, and with a full length portrait of King Charles I in his coronation robes, holding the sword of Justice in his right hand and the orb in his left. The Arms of England are at the top, with the Arms of Scotland and Ireland on the right and those of France on the left. The border has flowers, fruit, birds and insects intertwined. The charter, with

The charter of incorporation granted to the Clockmakers'
on 22nd August 1631 by King Charles I.

other records of the Company, is kept at the Guildhall Library where it may be viewed.

The Charter gave power to the Court to control the horological trade in the City of London and for 10 miles around. All apprentices were carefully and fully regulated and were bound to a Free Clockmaker. There was power to require them to produce a 'master piece' before the Court although this was not enforced. The Charter gave rigorous powers of protection for the members of the Company. There was power to inspect clocks coming into the City, including imported clocks, and if necessary to destroy them if they were of insufficient quality, or made by someone who had not served a full apprenticeship. This ensured that only the best designs and the best workmanship was accepted. All foreigners wishing to work in the trade had to be naturalised or to work with a recognised clockmaker and imported clocks were inspected and approved by the Clockmakers' Company. In this way, the Company could oversee the general direction of the clock making trade throughout the country. The public were protected against poor quality watches and clocks and bad workmanship. Huguenots and others fleeing from religious persecution in Europe had to become assimilated into the City to be able to work there. The waves of refugees brought with them fresh and innovative designs and techniques which combined with the English experience and traditions. At the same time there was also an influx of craftsmen in associated trades, such as cabinet making, enamelling and engraving, which provided expertise in all the crafts involved in clockmaking and which soon contributed to the 'Golden Age' of English clockmaking in the early 18th century.

The outstanding clockmakers were members of the Company and most became Master. Among many outstanding Masters are Edward East, watchmaker to King Charles I (1645), Henry Jones (1691), William Clement (1694), Charles Gretton (1700), Joseph Windmills (1702), Thomas Tompion (1703), Daniel Quare (1708), George Graham (1722), acknowledged to be the greatest horologist of his day and a most ingenious Mathematical Instrument Maker and B.L. Vulliamy (1821). Joseph Knibb, was a member of the Court of the Company in 1689 but unusually did not become Master. Four Astronomers

Thomas Tompion, the 'Father of English Watch and Clockmaking'. Master 1703.

Royal have served as Master and six Past Masters have served as Lord Mayor, including the past Lord Mayor, Alderman and Clockmaker, Sir Michael Savory (2005).

When the Company was incorporated the original members were Freemen of the Blacksmiths Company and other guilds, who had been able to obtain the consent of their parent Companies to join. Members also came from many of the other various associated branches of the trade and there was constant friction between the various companies and guilds over the boundaries of all their trades. Members of the Company, once they had obtained their Freedom, however, were not obliged to work as clockmakers but could practice any trade in the City.

The Clockmakers achieved a Livery in 1776 which then, and now, is limited to 300. There is no limit on the numbers of Freemen who may join the Company. Women were accorded an enlightened status by the Clockmakers from early times. A widow, sister or daughter of a deceased clockmaker was permitted to take apprentices through the Company as their deceased relative could. In 1676 Elizabeth Desbrow became the first female apprentice and the Court records show a number of female apprentices in the early eighteenth century. However, enlightenment did not continue and the first female Master was not installed until 2005. The colours of the Company are yellow and black.

The fortunes of the Company rose and fell with those of the City. It suffered very severe setbacks as a result of the plague in the City in the 1660's, followed by the Fire of London in 1666 when many clockmakers died and workshops were destroyed. During the subsequent periods of calm, trade revived and the Clockmakers flourished. Indeed , in 1697, the Company had built up sufficient funds to choose to invest by acquiring stock in the newly formed Bank of England and was the first City Company to do so. In 1947, when the Bank was nationalized, the Governor celebrated the fact that the Company had remained a stockholder without break until then and presented the Company with a silver bowl engraved *'Time with his scythe may sever links mature but Wisdom, Honour, Friendship — these endure 1697-1947'* (George White: The Clockmakers of London).

As set out in the Charter of 1631, the Company today is governed by a Master who is elected annually, three Wardens and a Court of not less than ten Assistants. The Company regulates its affairs through four Court meetings annually, which take place on or near the Quarter Days, the

Lady Day, Midsummer, Michaelmas and the Audit and Installation Court (previously the Christmas Court) which now, for convenience, takes place in January.

The Company does not have a Livery Hall of its own and over the years has met in many diverse places. There is a record that in 1642 the Clockmakers met at the Painter Stainers' Hall and gave them 'One Chamber Clock' for the use of the Hall. There are records of 17th century meetings in many different Livery Halls and taverns and finally in Guildhall.

As the Company did not have its own Hall, all its valuables, the silver, Charter, and various bonds, were placed in the Company's Strong Chest and were carried about the City by the current Master as was required. There were four keys to the chest which, for security, were held by the Master and the three Wardens who all had to be present to open the chest. Today the Company uses different Livery Halls for its meetings and functions but their offices are now located in Salters' Hall.

Clockmakers and those interested in horology and joining the Company may do so in various ways. The most usual method today is by redemption. Applicants invited to join the Company must be sponsored by two Liverymen, one of whom must be a member of the Court. An individual may join the Company by servitude, available to those who have served an apprenticeship, the original and traditional method of joining. Another method is by patrimony, so children born after their Father or Mother's admission to the Freedom may join when they become 21 years old. It is possible also to join by gift which is given to persons notable for achievement in or connected with horology, measurement of time, astronomy and kindred sciences or to persons who have rendered great service to the Company. They can also join Honoris Causa, awarded to a small number of persons of distinction in recognition of their achievements not necessarily connected with horology.

The Company's Coat of Arms.

A Freeman who is invited to become a Liveryman must first swear an oath in the Chamberlain's Court, thereby becoming a Freeman of the City of

London. In time he may serve as a Steward and become a member of the Court of Assistants from which the Wardens and Master are elected.

The Company has moved on from protecting the interests of its members and now encourages and promotes the development of horology and the measurement of time in all its aspects. The Company promotes modern clock and watch makers and the Clockmakers' Museum in Guildhall has a case of 20th and 21st century clocks. It makes grants to support training and the development of clockmaking and is expanding this part of its work and its charitable commitments. It arranges lectures, competitions, visits to horological collections, awards medals (most memorably their Tompion and Harrison medals) maintains memorials of past clockmakers and runs a social programme so that members may meet formally and informally to exchange ideas. The Clockmakers' Company today is responsible for the Clockmakers' Museum in Guildhall which houses the Company's fine collection of clocks and watches and is one of the best small museums in the country. The Company has links with the British Horological Institute and with the Antiquarian Horological Society.

An important example of its involvement in modern horology can be seen by reference to Dr. George Daniels' watch. Dr. Daniels was Master of the Clockmakers in 1980 and was the Tompion Gold Medallist in 1981. The watch, containing a patent fly-back chronograph and a four-minute tourbillon carriage, also includes his patented oil-free coaxial escapement now adopted by the celebrated Swiss Company Omega for the whole of their production.

Dr. Daniels' watch is in the Clockmakers' Museum.

A George Daniels wrist-watch.

As a Livery Company, it is also part of the City of London and so is involved with the many and varied activities of the City, such as the election of the Lord Mayor and sheriffs, attending the civic functions and sometimes participating in the Lord Mayor's Show.

The Company is delighted to be associated with the long overdue Memorial to John Harrison, celebrated in this book.

John Harrison, the Worshipful Company of Clockmakers and the Clockmakers' Museum

George White

John Harrison (1693-1776) was not a clock or watchmaker in the commercial sense. Perhaps that is why no attempt was ever made to enrol him as a Freeman of the Worshipful Company of Clockmakers, the London guild that oversaw the trade. Nevertheless, he spent more than half his life working in London and many who were Company Freemen, played significant parts in his career.

His first visit to London seems to have been in 1730. He had travelled from his home in Lincolnshire to discuss his ideas for finding the longitude at sea with the Astronomer Royal Edmond Halley (c. 1656-1742). The two met at Greenwich, but, because it was horological (rather than astronomical) advice that Harrison really needed, Halley redirected him to Fleet Street, to speak to George Graham (c.1674-1751).

Graham, a Quaker, was born in Cumberland, but had travelled to London in 1668 to become an apprentice through the Clockmakers' Company to Henry Aske (c.1655-c.1697) in St. Martin's Parish, Ludgate. He became a Freeman of the Company in 1695 and, having found employment in the workshop of the great Thomas Tompion (1639 -1713) in Water Lane, rose to become Tompion's successor and nephew by marriage. In 1723 he became Master of the Clockmakers' Company itself. By the time of Harrison's visit, Graham was running the most influential clock, watch and instrument-making business in Europe. Just as Microsoft today has largely created the language of worldwide computing through mass sales of software, so Graham dominated the scientific community and language of his day, through his instrument sales.

Halley assured Harrison that

> *"Mr. Graham was a very honest man, and would do me no harm, viz. as by pirating any Thing from me, but that on the contrary, would certainly do me Good if it was in his power"*

and such was the case. Graham not only made Harrison a loan at no

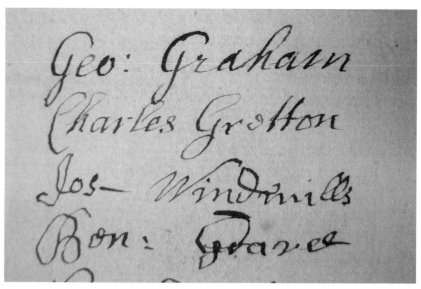

Important signatures on a document in the Museum.

interest, but became his principal adviser and champion. He remained so until his death in 1751.

When Harrison moved to the capital in 1737 and acquired premises in Leather Lane, his brother and assistant, James (1704-1776), seems to have accompanied him. James's time in London was, however, brief and thereafter Harrison turned to other highly skilled London-based craftsmen.

Principal amongst these was John Jefferys (fl. 1726-c.1753), who had been apprenticed through the Clockmakers' Company to Edward Jagger, obtaining his Freedom in 1726. Little work by Jefferys is identifiable today, largely because, as a *"repeating motion maker"*, he was part of the army of highly skilled makers of individual watch components which existed at the time in London. These supplied the "finishers" and retailers of completed instruments and seldom signed their work themselves.

"The Jefferys watch", made in 1753 for John Harrison's personal use.

Jefferys did however sign the complete watch he made to John Harrison's design and order in 1753. It contained four remarkable features, including the very early use of a bi-metallic strip for temperature compensation, and maintaining power, to prevent the watch from pausing as it was wound. It was to become the turning point in Harrison's scientific career.

It is no coincidence that when the Board of Longitude sought a highly skilled watchmaker to attend the 'disclosure' of Harrison's secrets, to transport his prize-winning fourth timekeeper to Greenwich and ultimately to reproduce it, they chose Larcum Kendall (1719-1790). Kendall had himself been apprenticed through the Clockmakers' to John Jefferys in 1735 for seven years. His copy of Harrison's work also achieved international fame, in the hands of Captain Cook (1728- 1779). Another to

attend the 'disclosure' was Thomas Mudge (c.1715- 1794) who had been apprenticed through the Company to George Graham in 1730 and in 1751 became his successor.

Harrison's first four marine timekeepers became the property of the state, on his receipt of the Longitude Prize money. But Harrison willed that, on his death, all the clocks and other artefacts that remained in his possession (including

The movement of Harrison's 5th marine timekeeper, completed in 1770 and tested by King George III in 1772.

his 1728 wooden regulator, many of his papers and most importantly, his fifth and last marine timekeeper), should go to his son William Harrison (1728- 1813). William in turn left them to his third wife Elizabeth, whom he married in 1786. On her death they were to pass to his grand daughter, Elizabeth (1797-1880). This they did, but not until 1865. Having no use for them, she at first offered them to the Patent Office Museum, forerunner of the Science Museum. After protracted and often irritable correspondence, in 1869 she sold them instead to Robert Napier (1791-1876), a wealthy collector, living in Gareloch, Scotland. It was after the sale of the Napier Collection in 1877 that the greater part of Harrison's personal effects, including the regulator and "H5", passed into the hands of the Clockmakers' Company. They were placed on display in the Clockmakers' Museum at Guildhall, which had been founded in 1813 and had been opened permanently to the public in 1873.

The excitement of acquiring and displaying so much of Harrison's work, turned the Company's attention to the great man's grave in Hampstead Churchyard. In 1879, it was decided to restore it, but as it had *"so far succumbed to the influences of time and weather",* it proved necessary to reconstruct it instead. This was done at the expense of the Company, in Ketton and Spinkwell stone, with Sicilian marble panels.

Thus, the Clockmakers' Company, whose connection with Harrison in his lifetime was indirect, has become the owner of much of his property, the voluntary guardian of his tomb and, in 2006 through the generosity of its membership (and others), the sponsor of his memorial in Westminster Abbey. In addition to a recently acquired half-scale replica of Harrison's first Marine Timekeeper, its Museum now contains two of Harrison's original wooden longcase movements (those made in 1713 and c. 1726) and one complete longcase (his personal regulator, made in 1728). With them (by kind permission of the Brethren of Hull Trinity House), is the hugely important "Jefferys" watch. Most exciting of all, is Harrison's fifth and last timekeeper, once personally tested by King George III, which the Company has now owned for a longer period than Harrison himself.

The Clockmakers' Museum is maintained by the Clockmakers' Museum and Educational Trust, whose purpose is horological education of all kinds. The Museum can be visited (entry free), at Guildhall Library Aldermanbury, EC2. It is open from 9.30 a.m. until 4.30 p.m. every day except Sundays and Bank Holidays.

Beyond The Bench – A Glimpse into The Essence of Genius

Andrew King

John Harrison was a driven man. Driven by a total commitment to his life's work, almost a divine mission to reach out for perfection.

Harrison had a true understanding of Newtonian thought, together with an exceptional talent and a remarkable intuition for lateral thought and analysis. But who is this man who solved the centuries old problem of the Discovery of Longitude at Sea; a problem which had tested the greatest minds? What do we know of the man beyond the bench?

Harrison wrote copiously on the two subjects he pursued throughout his life. Horology, the quest for precision timekeeping on land and at sea, and music, the quest for a perfection of scale based on mathematical formulae. Harrison by his own admission was,

"...no great lover of music, viz any further than for or touching its chief intent and so as it had pleased God to give me a good ear..."

It must have been the sense of perfect pitch that enabled Harrison to develop the mathematical theory where he was able to hear the musical scale he devised, a scale divided into as many as twenty five parts, as opposed to the classical acceptance of twelve. A determination to find perfect tone through perfect pitch. It was in the church at Barrow where Harrison achieved a standard which according to some exceeded anything then known. Harrison went further, in the tuning of musical instruments and church bells, both with the instruments themselves and the monochords he pioneered as tuning standards.

It was with church bells and from being a bellringer himself that Harrison began to understand the properties of a mass oscillating in an exaggerated arc, translating this experience into the motion of a pendulum. This lateral deduction from peripheral experiences is the epitome of Harrison's thought patterns and progression; a derivative process that he followed throughout his life, always maintaining that everything he did or made depended on its precursor,

"Now these discoveries ... could never have been made if I had not had that other machine which I made sometime before I set about to make any of these Longitude machines, viz my Pendulum Clock; nor had one good cause towards such truth as the Long Pendulum Clock ... been known if I had not made my first machine for the 'Longitude'; and however these discoveries may be looked upon, they certainly are greater in themselves than that of the Longitude thereafter is likely to be....."

Harrison's achievement first with fixed pendulum clocks and then precision watches is as brilliant as it is unique. His earliest surviving writings from when he was still living in Lincolnshire display a scientific mind far in advance of his contempories. His paper dating from 1730 ranks amongst the most important scientific papers of the 18th century. In this paper Harrison describes the clock he has made for which he claims a rate of to within one second a month including definition of barometric error, matters not addressed or exceeded until the following century. The testing methods therein described are again very much in advance of their time. This is but just an introduction to the main purpose — a proposal for what was to become the world's first successful marine timekeeper, the Sea Clock H1. The Sea Clocks H1, 2 and 3 represent at least twenty five years work. Whilst the first was the only one tested at sea, the later two never left the workshop. The last of the large Sea Clocks, H3, by far the most complex but with no hope of being a successful timekeeper, proved to be the most important. With its two large slow beating circular balances and just a single balance spring Harrison had a fundamental problem which on the one hand resulted in the failure of the timekeeper but, paradoxically, was to be his salvation because it led him directly into research into springs and springing which he described to the Board of Longitude in 1746 :

"That after much time and thought spent in making many new Experiments upon Springs and in various Methods of tempering them, ...he has at last gained so much knowledge in the properties of Springs..."

It is interesting to note that in 1763 Harrison magnanimously admitted failure to achieve success with H3 as a timekeeper :

"...I had an endless trouble with a small part (the balance spring) of my third machine ... but never could thereby rightly conquer it."

H3 unwittingly became a research vehicle which was crucial when Harrison investigated watch making and achieved ultimate success. This first watch designed by Harrison was made by John Jefferys and was developed from the general concept of a watch of the period but incorporating most of the ground breaking innovations which were to be utilized in the next watch, H4. These days, the 'Jefferys Watch', completed in 1753, tends to be sidelined in the context of Harrison's achievements. Without doubt the Jefferys Watch should be brought centre stage as the fourth marine timekeeper, the very first to be successfully represented by a watch. In the only known portrait of Harrison he proudly and defiantly holds this Watch, arguable the greatest break-through in his life, with the recalcitrant H3, the last of the Sea

Clocks, smouldering in the shadows.

The Jefferys Watch reportedly performed very well when tested at sea but in 1759 Harrison produced a completely new timekeeper. Much bigger, to be able to encompass all the required features, the entire watch reveals Harrison's progressive thinking and what became a truly unique and pioneering design. H4 set startling new standards of timekeeping. The London trade was left in shock. By 1730, Harrison had set a standard of timekeeping for clocks far in advance of anything known; thirty years later, by 1760, Harrison had re-written the rule book once again — this time for watchmakers. The two sea trials of H4 to the West Indies proved a technical triumph. Not content with this, Harrison quietly developed an even more advanced pendulum clock system for which he predicted a rate of 3 to 4 seconds a year. Although never completed by Harrison, recent research indicates that Harrison's claims were achievable and further this precision of rate is just about the ultimate for a pendulum in free air.

In summary, Harrison achieved two significant break-throughs. First, by 1730, he proved that it was possible to reach a precision, up to then unheard of, approaching a rate which would satisfy the most demanding requirements for the determination of Longitude. Second, with H4 he provided both the scale and precision of rate for what eventually became the marine 'chronometer'.

If one per cent is the inspiration over toil that defines genius then John Harrison's life of dedication to the cause of pioneering precision timekeeping on land and at sea remains the perfect definition. And in addition he remains one of the founding fathers of the Industrial Revolution.

A Fitting and Timely Memorial

Jonathan Betts

*H*arrison's memorial is situated in the floor of the Abbey, close to the centre of the nave. It is in an important and prominent position, richly deserved by the man who solved the greatest scientific problem of his age, the finding of Longitude at sea. Harrison's prize-winning timekeeper H4 — "The Mona Lisa of Horology" as clockmakers like to call it — not only provided the solution, but formed the basis for all mechanical precision watches which followed; Harrison's was a monumental achievement.

As told elsewhere in this book, Harrison had the support of a number of his scientific and academic contemporaries in seeking reward for his endeavours. One in particular, George Graham (c.1674-1751), the most prominent watchmaker and instrument maker of his day, lies just a metre away, alongside his former business partner, Thomas Tompion (1639-1713), "the Father of English Watchmaking". Alongside Tompion

HERE LIES THE BODY
OF M.ᴿ THO TOMPION
WHO DEPARTED THIS
LIFE THE 20ᵀᴴ OF
NOVEMBER J7J3 IN THE
J5ᵀᴴ YEAR OF HIS AGE

ALSO THE BODY OF
GEORGE GRAHAM OF LONDON
WATCHMAKER AND F. R. S,
WHOSE CURIOUS INVENTIONS
DO HONOUR TO Yᵉ BRITISH GENIUS
WHOSE ACCURATE PERFORMANCES
ARE Yᵉ STANDARD OF MECHANICS SKILL
HE DIED Yᵉ XVI OF NOVEMBER MDCCLI
IN THE LXXVIII YEAR OF HIS AGE

The tomb of Thomas Tompion and George Graham, a metre to the west of Harrison's memorial. Graham had been one of Harrison's most loyal supporters.

and Graham lies the body of David Livingstone (1813-1873), the celebrated missionary and explorer, a man very much at the 'sharp end' of terrestrial navigation and one who relied on the chronometer in determining his position when in the wilds of Africa. Then, just a metre or so to the north of Harrison's memorial is the tomb of the great 19th century civil engineer Thomas Telford (1757-1834). Harrison is thus in highly appropriate and distinguished company.

Cut in Purbeck Grub (the brown limestone often mistakenly referred to as 'Purbeck marble'), the John Harrison memorial reflects two elements which were central to the great man's achievement: Timekeeping and *Longitude* (one's east-west position on the Earth). Harrison dedicated the majority of his life to creating a solution to the Longitude problem and, after he had finally gained the celebrated Longitude prize money, he became known as John 'Longitude' Harrison, distinguishing him from lesser mortals of the same name. It is this soubriquet with which he is identified on the memorial.

The design for the John Harrison memorial. In Purbeck grub, the 'bimetallic meridian line' is in steel and brass and has the longitude from Greenwich engraved upon it..

Meridians and Longitude

Running across the tablet is an inlaid metal line marking the *meridian* of the memorial. Meridians are the imaginary lines, running north-south over the surface of the Earth, from pole to pole, and between which longitude is measured. Since 1884 (when a resolution was agreed at the International Meridian Conference in Washington) the Greenwich meridian has been *The Prime Meridian* of the world, the one upon which, over the years, the various Astronomers Royal made their observations and the one from which all other meridians have been measured, internationally.

The line in the tablet is actually formed of two metal strips, one of brass and one of steel, running in parallel. This represents one of John Harrison's truly great inventions, the *bimetal*, a temperature-sensitive device which is still very much in use today in thermostats, kettle switches and a multitude of other applications. The tablet's meridian, its line of longitude, runs directly through the name of HARRISON, just as longitude itself ran centrally right through Harrison's life as his ever present preoccupation, his *raison d'etre*. Reflecting this concern with precise longitude determination, the memorial's meridian line has the exact longitude of the memorial, its angular distance west from the Greenwich meridian, inscribed upon it.

A Longitude Problem

Surprisingly, given the sophisticated navigation equipment available to us these days, finding the figure for this longitude turned out not to be as simple as one might think. Ironically, and perhaps highly appropriately, determining the longitude of the tablet — like much of Harrison's own work — proved complicated.

The obvious instrument to use in the 21st century is a GPS (Global Positioning System) receiver. Thanks to the super-accurate atomic clocks employed in the satellites (yes, even today finding longitude ultimately depends on precision timekeepers) one's longitude can be determined to within a very small fraction of a degree on the surface of the Earth. However, when finding the longitude of Harrison's memorial from Greenwich one is faced with a quandary as, historically, Greenwich, has got more than one 'prime meridian'. In fact at the Observatory there are *three* Greenwich meridians concerned with this story.

The meridian established by the third Astronomer Royal, James Bradley, in 1750, was the one used by all the subsequent Astronomers Royal (including Harrison's nemesis, Nevil Maskelyne), up until 1851. In that year, the seventh Astronomer Royal, George Biddell Airy, founded a new meridian, five metres or so to the East of Bradley's. Bradley's meridian and its associated telescope still had their uses, but Airy's new telescope, termed a 'transit circle', was more powerful and accurate. It was Airy's meridian which was adopted internationally in 1884 as the prime meridian of the world, for all charts and maps, and as the basis for the world's time zone system.

In 1984, exactly a century later, the U.S.A.'s Global Positioning System was launched. To conform as closely as practicable to existing charts, the system was nominally designed to use Greenwich as the basis for its reference meridian. However, owing to a number of tiny technical errors, introduced locally when the system was developed, the GPS default reference meridian does not quite coincide with Airy's; currently it is about 100 metres east of Airy's (conveniently marked by a litter bin in Greenwich Park!). In terms of the modern system itself, this discrepancy is irrelevant, as the actual location of the reference meridian no longer depends on the exact position of Airy's telescope.   But, as we wished to inscribe Harrison's memorial with its exact longitude from Greenwich, we had to decide: which Greenwich meridian to use?

Bradley's Meridian

After due consideration, it was Bradley's we chose as being the most

The Meridian Building at the Royal Observatory, Greenwich. Bradley's meridian, from which Nevil Maskelyne rated H4 in 1766, is on the right with black shuttering. Airy's prime meridian is seen a few metres to the left, attended by visitors.

appropriate. After all, it was this meridian which was in use in Harrison's day, and it was this meridian from which Nevil Maskelyne determined the time and set the Observatory's clocks by which he checked the performance of H4 when it was on trial at Greenwich in the 1760s. Also, Bradley's meridian coincides with the British Ordnance Survey's reference meridian, for which there is conveniently an option on GPS receivers. So it was only necessary to select this (OS/GB36) when using the GPS receiver and a direct reading would be given….if only a signal could be picked up by the receiver in the nave of the Abbey.

Unfortunately, owing to the heavy stone walls and vaulting, a signal was not found, in spite of repeated trials, and it was necessary to estimate as accurately as possible a place outside the building, due north of where the memorial was located. This provided the necessary reading of 000° 07'35"WEST. Just to double check this figure, the large scale mapping service of the Ordnance Survey was used to identify the 'Northings' and 'Eastings' (the OS equivalents of Longitude and Latitude) of the position. This was then converted to Latitude and Longitude (GPS meridian) from which the longitude from Bradley's meridian could be deduced…. and the figure was finally confirmed.

*T*he Memorial's Meridian

Marking the memorial's meridian line also proved more complicated than expected. It is known that the axis of the Abbey does not exactly conform to the cardinal points of the compass. The nave does not quite run East/ West, and the transepts do not quite run North/South. So the meridian line on the tablet, which must run due North/South (otherwise it would not be a proper meridian) needed to appear slightly skewed on the tablet. But by how much?

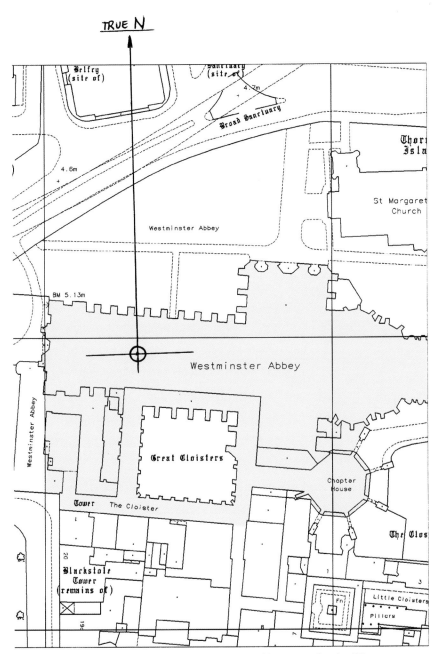

Ordnance Survey 'Siteplan', showing the position of the memorial in the Abbey nave, with True North marked.

With the help of Professor Stuart Malin, former Head of Geomagnetism at the British Geological Survey, true North, in relation to the Abbey nave, was found using two methods. Firstly, observations were made by compass in and around the site of the memorial (carefully avoiding Telford's memorial which is a solid iron plate) and the necessary correction applied (2 degrees, 17 arc-minutes eastward) to derive true North from magnetic North. By coincidence, it appears that this is almost certainly the method chosen by Edmond Halley, when he was asked to establish the orientation for new churches in 1712-1715 (J.R. Ali and P. Cunich, Astronomy and Geophysics, 46, 2005). The figure for true North in the Abbey was then checked by measurement off a large scale (1:1250) Ordnance Survey 'Siteplan', making the necessary 1 degree, 28 arc-minutes westward grid correction. The two figures, which both agreed within one degree of their mean, indicated that the line on the tablet should run 7 degrees West of the North/South axis of the Abbey, and it is at this angle that the 'bimetallic meridian' is placed. Harrison's inscription on the tablet is run parallel to this meridian, rather than the 'North/South axis' of the Abbey, emphasizing again the importance of longitude in the story.

Creation of the Memorial

Many people have contributed to the creation of this timely and fitting memorial. It was made and designed by the artists Gary Breeze and Joanna Migdal, with input from John Burton (Purcell Miller Tritton LLP), the Westminster Abbey Fabric Committee and the Dean and Chapter, amongst others.

It is a fine, very carefully considered design and very welcome among the horological fraternity who have long felt that Harrison's achievement needed better acknowledgement. It is not, of course, the great man's tomb, John Harrison was buried in the graveyard of St John's church in Hampstead, North London, and there is a fine monument

Harrison's tomb in Hampstead churchyard, shown in its original form in a fine watercolour of 1843.

to him there. Harrison has naturally always been held in high esteem by his fellow horologists, and, as told elsewhere in this book, the Worshipful Company of Clockmakers took the trouble to reconstruct this much-decayed monument in 1879.

Harrison's tomb after its restoration and rebuilding by the Clockmakers' Company in 1879, shown in a photograph probably taken soon after the restoration.

There have been one or two other 'memorials' of various kinds. 1966 saw the publication of Colonel Humphrey Quill's biography of

Harrison, and in 1976 the bicentenary of Harrison's death was marked by a splendid exhibition at the National Maritime Museum. That same year Colonel Quill unveiled a photographic copy of the portrait, by Thomas King, at Harrison's childhood church, Holy Trinity at Barrow on Humber. Then, as a result of Quill's championship, the local Church of England school at Barrow was named, in honour of the town's most famous son, *The John Harrison School*.

In 1993, to mark the tercentenary of Harrison's birth, the whole of the Royal Observatory's historic galleries at Greenwich were refurbished, including fine new displays for Harrison's famous marine timekeepers, H1 – H4 and the publication of the little biographical booklet *Harrison*. That year also saw the seminal Harvard Longitude Symposium, organised by Will Andrewes, at which so much of Harrison's achievement was discussed and celebrated. This, in turn, led to the writing of Dava Sobel's best-seller *Longitude* and several television documentaries, a film, and a theatre play based on the story: at last John Harrison was a household name. There was even a 'millennium' tribute paid to him by the London Borough of Greenwich, when one of the major dual carriageways on the Greenwich peninsula (home to the controversial 'millennium dome'), was named *John Harrison Way*.

There was once a time when his admirers might seriously have wondered whether, in spite of his great achievement, Harrison's name would really be remembered in perpetuity. But with the Abbey's new memorial we can finally rest assured the name of John Harrison will never be forgotten.

Biographies of the Contributors

Mr. William J.H. Andrewes is a Museum Consultant specializing in the history of scientific instruments and time measurement. He edited and contributed to the influential 'The Quest for Longitude', the proceedings of the Harvard Longitude Symposium, 1993.

Mr. Jonathan Betts FSA, FBHI, is Senior Specialist, Horology, at the National Maritime Museum, Greenwich. He is a Liveryman of the Clockmakers' Company and was its first Harrison Medallist.

Mr. Joe Buxton served as a regular Army Officer in the Grenadier Guards, and spent 20 years in the Wine Shipping business. He is now Clerk to the Clockmakers' Company.

Mr. Andrew King is a horologist who has researched the life and work of John Harrison over many years. He is a Liveryman of the Clockmakers' Company.

Dava Sobel, the second Harrison Medallist, is the author of 'Longitude', 'Galileo's Daughter' and 'The Planets'; as well as co-author, with W.J.H. Andrewes, of 'The Illustrated Longitude'.

Dr. Anne Stevenson, of Durham, is a poet, critic and biographer, most notably of Sylvia Plath.

Dr. John C. Taylor is an inventor. He is a Liveryman of the Clockmakers' Company and is currently designing and constructing a new type of clock for his Cambridge College, Corpus Christi, of which he is an Honorary Fellow.

Mrs. Diana Uff, LLM, FKC was Master of the Clockmakers' Company for 2005, during which most of the arrangements for the Harrison memorial were made. Mrs. Uff was the first woman Master.

Sir George White Bt, FSA is a Past Master of the Worshipful Company of Clockmakers and has been Keeper of its Museum since 1988. He has published on Horological matters.

Sir Arnold Wolfendale, FRS was the 14th Astronomer Royal. He is an Honorary Liveryman of the Clockmakers' Company and President of the Antiquarian Horological Society.

Bibliography and Acknowledgements

The illustrations have been taken from a number of sources and the contributors are grateful for permission to re-publish them here. Such gratitude is accorded to:

The Royal Society
The National Maritime Museum
The Worshipful Company of Clockmakers
The Dean and Chapter of Westminster Abbey
Jeffrey L. Ward Graphic Design (the map of H-4's 2nd voyage)
Simon Stacey and Sarah Stacey (the Gould image)
Dean and Chapter of Westminster
Science and Society Picture Gallery

There are many books which relate to the story of John Harrison. Of particular relevance are those with which the particular authors of the articles here have been associated, most notably:

'The Quest for Longitude', Edited by William J.H. Andrewes; the Proceedings of the Longitude Symposium, Cambridge, Mass., 1993. Publishers: Harvard University. ISBN 0-96-44329-0-0

'The Clockmakers of London'. George White, 1998. Printed by The Midas Press. ISBN 0-95-12978-1-3

'The Illustrated Longitude', Dava Sobel and William J.H. Andrewes, 1998. Publishers, Walker and Company, New York. ISBN 0-8027-1344-0

'Longitude', Dava Sobel, 1995. Publishers, Walker and Co. New York Publishing Company Inc. ISBN 1-85702-502-4

'The Clockmakers Library', compiled by John Bromley, 1977. Philip Wilson Publishers Ltd. ISBN 0-85667-033-2

'Westminster Abbey : Official Guide', 1997, Dean and Chapter of Westminster. ISBN 0-7117-0381-7

'Some Account of the Worshipful Company of Clockmakers' (1881) S.E. Atkins and W.H. Overall.

The Harrison Memorial Fund

Joe Buxton

The 'Harrison Memorial' has been funded by way of an Appeal sent to all members of the Worshipful Company of Clockmakers and others. The funds raised in excess of those associated with the Memorial will be devoted to two worthy causes:

- The provision of 'Harrison Bursaries' to help keep clockmakers-to-be in their studies, and
- The Clockmakers' Museum in The Guildhall

The Museum is described briefly in the article by the Keeper, Sir George White Bt. FSA; the educational aspect is looked after by the distinguished clockmaker Mr. David Poole, FSA – Mr. Poole will be Master of the Worshipful Company of Clockmakers in 2007.

The Company wishes to build up support for both 'projects' and to this end welcomes further donations (to be sent to the Clerk at The Worshipful Company of Clockmakers, Salters' Hall, Fore Street, London E2Y 5DE, please). Cheques to be made payable to 'The Clockmakers' Charitable Fund'.

Such contributions will act as a continuing tribute to John Harrison.

Significant donations have been made by many, including those listed at the end of the book. We acknowledge their support with gratitude.

We are particularly grateful to the following donors
(list complete to mid-February, 2006)

The Ogden Trust

The Antiquarian Horological Society

The National Physical Laboratory

Mr. Garth Hamp-Gopsill

Smith of Derby Group Ltd.

Mrs. Mary Harrison-Drummond

Mr. Nicholas Smith

Dava Sobel

Charles Frodsham & Co. Ltd.

Mr. Geoffrey Heywood MBE

Physics Department, Durham University

Dr. George Daniels MBE

Dr. John C. Taylor HonDEng

Mr. John Carrington

Dr. Michael D. Sanderson

Mr. Andrew Crisford

Mrs. Diana Uff

Sir Arnold Wolfendale FRS

Mr. Anthony Woodburn

William and Catherine Andrewes

Maj. Gen. David Pennefather CB OBE

Mrs. Isobel Lattimore

The Royal Society

Mr. Philip Whyte

Mr. Raymond Mellor